Moving Day

Written and Illustrated by
Dionna L. Hayden

LUCKY BOOTS

Copyright © 2015 Dionna L. Hayden. All Rights Reserved.

Text and Illustrations by Dionna L. Hayden | Design and Layout by Pink Elephant Graphic Design | Published by Lucky Boots

No part of this book may be reproduced in any form, stored in a retrieval system, or transmitted in any form by any means— electronic, **mechanical**, photocopy, recording, or otherwise—without prior written permission of author or publisher except for the use of brief quotations in a book review.

Made in the U.S.A. - First Edition 2015   Premium Paperback ISBN: 978-0-9964567-3-9

www.cfrkids.com

To "Boots" and "Lucky",
thank you for seeing the potential and helping
a little girl believe it was possible.

Love, Didi

Join the Journey

One of the greatest gifts parents can give their children is time. One of the best ways parents can share time with their children is through reading. The ability to read is a critical skill for social and academic development. Reading helps individuals obtain knowledge. Throughout her book series, The Cookie-Flower Rock Kids, Dionna L. Hayden, provides parents and children with wonderful literary resources that make reading a fun, informative, and imaginative activity.

In addition to providing great reads that can be added to any child's library, The Cookie-Flower Rock Kids honors children by amplifying their voice and highlighting the trials and triumphs of pre-adolescent lived experiences. Throughout the series, Dionna L. Hayden, uses vibrant illustrations and perky plots to draw attention to social concerns that humanity has grappled with from time immemorial (e.g., love; loss; belonging; affirmation; inclusion; competition; etc.). With artistic flare and a mother's discernment, Dionna L. Hayden has apprehended the dynamics of these issues and interpreted them through the lens of children.

> "*The Cookie-Flower Rock Kids series captures youth social dynamics along with its challenges, consequences, celebratory moments, and caveats.*"

Most unique about The Cookie-Flower Rock Kids series experience is the instructive trek encountered in each book. Through illustrative genius and witty dialogue, readers engage relevant interpersonal issues such as bullying. Readers are then guided to palpable solutions that can be applied to life situations irrespective of time and place. Critical lessons are conveyed in the stories that promote the acquisition and development of humanitarian values (e.g., acceptance; forgiveness; respect; sharing, etc.). Quite masterfully and light-heartedly, The Cookie-Flower Rock Kids series captures youth social dynamics along with its challenges, consequences, celebratory moments, and caveats.

All in all, The Cookie-Flower Rock Kids extends an invitation to examine "the world of children". It helps demystify—for adults—the entry points of real-life topics that can be difficult for children to understand. Parents, in particular, will rejoice to know that The Cookie-Flower Rock Kids series has made it a bit easier and enjoyable to answer tough questions that children often hurl in their direction. The entire family will be delighted to read, wonder, reason, laugh, and smile as they learn how to negotiate and navigate life through the experiences of The Cookie-Flower Rock Kids!

Marcus L. Arrington, Ed.D.
Young, Anointed and Empowered Project
Milwaukee, WI

Meet the Cookie-Flower Rock Kids. Twin sisters, Kyla and Devin, and little brother Kris-Alex!

Kyla is a sunny girl with many dreams and a great love for art.

One of her dreams is to become an artist and share beautiful creations with the world.

Devin is an undercover rockstar who spends much of her time reading her favorite books, practicing her mean drum solo and dancing to her favorite tunes!

Kris-Alex is a high-energy kid genius who enjoys playing sports, learning new languages and winding down to computer games.

Today is moving day for the family. After living in the same neighborhood for many years, it was time to move to a different home.

Mommy and Daddy packed everything they owned in boxes. Then the movers placed their belongings on the moving truck to take to the new location.

Kyla frowned, Devin refused to calm down and Kris was downright grumpy! Leaving their many friends and memories was just too hard. It seemed so unfair!

"Where will I pick pretty flowers?" cried Kyla.

"Where will we go to school?" inquired Devin.

"Who's going to play with me?" whined Kris-Alex.

Before leaving to their new home, the trio waived goodbye one last time.

"Goodbye old home. Goodbye old neighborhood." the children sadly expressed.

When the family arrived at their new neighborhood, the kids were pleasantly surprised because it was beautiful!

Freshly bloomed flowers decorated all the lawns.

Friendly neighborhood children gleefully played at the nearby park.

The best part was their new home. It was very nice and big with plenty of room.

After the movers had moved all of the family's belongings inside the house, it was time to unpack.

Every child took their own box and began unpacking beginning with some of their favorite things.

Kyla unpacked her art supplies, doll and ballet magazines.

Devin unpacked her drums, journals and gym shoes while Kris-Alex unpacked his radio, ant farm and toy fire truck.

After spending much of the day unpacking, Mommy and Daddy took the kids out for some ice cream.

Kyla picked strawberry.
Devin picked vanilla.
Kris-Alex picked chocolate.

While at the ice cream parlor, the parents talked to the trio concerning the move and why it was a good and needed change for their family.

After the discussion, the children began to get excited about the move and started imagining all the great new things it would bring.

Later at bedtime, all the children rested peacefully thinking about enjoying their new home and new neighborhood while making new friends and memories.

"Goodnight new house. Goodnight new neighborhood." the children lightly whispered.

With a sigh of relief before falling fast asleep, all were comforted with
one last thought...
Change is good!

Parent Soapbox

 ### Change Is Good

The day my husband Kyle and I became parents was the day our twins Kyla and Devin were born. 2 1/2 years later, we were graced with our son Kristian Alexander. Hours after becoming new parents, my husband shared some profound parenting insight that I never forgot. He stated that every day our children grow older, would be one day less they would be in our nest. Since we knew they were not going to remain children forever, it was best to take all the necessary steps to prepare all of us for this unavoidable change.

Change is constant and always happening. With change comes the opportunity to learn or experience something new. Although some changes are not very pleasant, they too give us opportunities to grow and mature. So when change happens, it's best for us to adapt the best way possible. The more flexible we are, the more we can benefit from life's changes that occurs.

Children come into this world as clean slates in need of guidance and training until they reach adulthood. In that span of time, our children will experience countless changes; the sooner they learn to adapt, the better. So as parents and guardians, it's really important for us to teach them how according to what they are able to grasp. Maybe your family is moving, preparing for a new baby or your child is attending school for the first time. Whatever the situation may be, this book can be a great way to spring board the subject at hand; making your reading this book help spark a love of life learning for your child and achieving quality time as a family.

www.ingramcontent.com/pod-product-compliance
Lightning Source LLC
Chambersburg PA
CBHW042143290426
44110CB00002B/99